Max Packs a Box

Practicing the KS Sound

Whitney Walker

Rosen
PHONICS
READERS

Rosen
Classroom™

Max is moving.
He packs a box.

Max has many books!
Max packs his books.

Max has a fox.
Max packs his fox.

Max has clocks.
Max packs his clocks.

Max will need socks.
Max packs his socks.

Max has rocks.

He packs his rocks.

Max makes snacks.
What snacks should Max make?

Max packs snacks
in a lunch box.

Max packs forks for the snacks.

There are two trucks.
Max walks the box to the trucks.

Max looks at his watch.
Time to go!